FAITH | WORD | OPEN DOORS | CHANGE

Journal Start Date: _____

KINGDOM NEWS TODAY
Publication Services, LLC

MEDITATIONS FOR THE WRITER

*"And it came to pass, that when Jehudi had read three or four leaves,
he cut it with the penknife, and cast it into the fire that was on the
hearth, until all the roll was consumed in the fire that was on the
hearth. Then the word of the Lord came to Jeremiah, after that the king
had burned the roll, and the words which Baruch wrote at the mouth of
Jeremiah, saying, Take thee again another roll, and write in it all the
former words that were in the first roll, which Jehoiakim the king of
Judah hath burned."*
Jeremiah 36:23, 27-28

Writing is a powerful, multifaceted tool that empowers us to express, release, and heal. It helps us to put our thoughts on paper, sort out our emotions, write our prayers, and record our days. Each word holds a key to making sense of it all.

Writing is a creative act that inspires us to imagine worlds, pen poetic verses, connect through storytelling, document dreams, and capture plans and visions. Each sentence contains a path to understanding and insight as it unfolds a blueprint that unlocks destinies.

Writing was often used in the Bible. Many prophets and scribes wrote the word of the Lord. David's psalms gave us poetical encouragement, while King Solomon wrote words of wisdom. Perhaps the Holy Spirit is the best author of them all since every scripture was God-breathed for instruction, doctrine, reproof, and as an invitation to know God's will for our lives.

Writing establishes a sense of permanence. When we write, we can always go back and reread the words, relive the memories, and remember the dreams. With God's word, it cannot be bound, hindered, or destroyed.

In the scriptures above, the Hebrew word for leaves is *deleth*[1]. It means a door, gate, or the doors of heaven. Each page of our writing is a door to deliverance. Writing can set us or our readers free.

We overcome the enemy by the blood of the Lamb and the word of our testimonies. We bring glory to God when we tell our stories. They plant seeds of hope and breakthrough. Each story shows that He brought us out so we could bring others in to see the goodness of the Lord in the land of the living.

We must have the *faith* to stand on God's *word* to write the story that will *open doors* to *change*.

Now is the time to write yourself and others out.

---

[1] "H1817 - deleth - Strong's Hebrew Lexicon (KJV)." Blue Letter Bible. Accessed 20 Sep, 2020
https://www.blueletterbible.org//lang/lexicon/lexicon.cfm?Strongs=H1817&t=KJV

"Your ears shall hear a word behind you, saying,
"This is the way, walk in it,"
Whenever you turn to the right hand
Or whenever you turn to the left."
Isaiah 30:21 NKJV

FAITH

"God is in the midst of her; she shall not be moved: God shall help her, and that right early."
Psalm 46:5

_____

_____

_____

_____

_____

_____

_____

_____

_____

_____

_____

_____

_____

_____

_____

_____

_____

_____

_____

_____

Writing My Way Out

WORD

"But he answered and said, It is written, Man shall not live by bread alone, but by every word that proceedeth out of the mouth of God."
Matthew 4:4

_____

_____

_____

_____

_____

_____

_____

_____

_____

_____

_____

_____

_____

_____

_____

_____

_____

_____

_____

_____

_____

Writing My Way Out

OPEN DOORS

"And the key of the house of David will I lay upon his shoulder; so he shall open, and none shall shut; and he shall shut, and none shall open."
Isaiah 22:22

_____

_____

_____

_____

_____

_____

_____

_____

_____

_____

_____

_____

_____

_____

_____

_____

_____

_____

Writing My Way Out

CHANGE

"Jesus saith unto him, Rise, take up thy bed, and walk."
John 5:8

Writing My Way Out

FAITH

"Through faith also Sara herself received strength to conceive seed, and was delivered of a child when she was past age, because she judged him faithful who had promised."
Hebrew 11:11

_____

_____

_____

_____

_____

_____

_____

_____

_____

_____

_____

_____

_____

_____

_____

_____

_____

_____

Writing My Way Out

WORD

"For the word of God is quick, and powerful, and sharper than any twoedged sword, piercing even to the dividing asunder of soul and spirit, and of the joints and marrow, and is a discerner of the thoughts and intents of the heart."
Hebrews 4:12

_____

_____

_____

_____

_____

_____

_____

_____

_____

_____

_____

_____

_____

_____

_____

_____

Writing My Way Out

OPEN DOORS

"For a great door and effectual is opened unto me, and there are many adversaries."
1 Corinthians 16:9

_____

_____

_____

_____

_____

_____

_____

_____

_____

_____

_____

_____

_____

_____

_____

_____

_____

_____

_____

_____

Writing My Way Out

CHANGE

"Write the vision, and make it plain upon tables, that he may run that readeth it."

Habakkuk 2:2

_____

_____

_____

_____

_____

_____

_____

_____

_____

_____

_____

_____

_____

_____

_____

_____

_____

Writing My Way Out

FAITH

"For she said, If I may touch but his clothes, I shall be whole."
Mark 5:8

_____

_____

_____

_____

_____

_____

_____

_____

_____

_____

_____

_____

_____

_____

_____

_____

_____

_____

_____

_____

Writing My Way Out

WORD

"In the beginning was the Word, and the Word was with God, and the Word was God."

John 1:1

Writing My Way Out

OPEN DOORS

"I know thy works: behold, I have set before thee an open door, and no man can shut it: for thou hast a little strength, and hast kept my word, and hast not denied my name."
Revelations 3:8

_____

_____

_____

_____

_____

_____

_____

_____

_____

_____

_____

_____

_____

_____

_____

_____

_____

_____

_____

Writing My Way Out

CHANGE

"The woman then left her waterpot, and went her way into the city, and saith to the men, Come, see a man, which told me all things that ever I did: is not this the Christ?"

John 4:28-29

_____

_____

_____

_____

_____

_____

_____

_____

_____

_____

_____

_____

_____

_____

_____

_____

_____

_____

_____

_____

Writing My Way Out

_____

_____

_____

_____

_____

_____

_____

_____

_____

_____

_____

_____

_____

_____

_____

_____

_____

_____

_____

_____

_____

_____

_____

_____

_____

_____

_____

FAITH

"He staggered not at the promise of God through unbelief; but was strong in faith, giving glory to God;"
Romans 4:20

_____

_____

_____

_____

_____

_____

_____

_____

_____

_____

_____

_____

_____

_____

_____

_____

_____

_____

Writing My Way Out

WORD

"The centurion answered and said, Lord, I am not worthy that thou shouldest come under my roof: but speak the word only, and my servant shall be healed."
Matthew 8:8

_____

_____

_____

_____

_____

_____

_____

_____

_____

_____

_____

_____

_____

_____

_____

_____

Writing My Way Out

OPEN DOORS

"And suddenly there was a great earthquake, so that the foundations of the prison were shaken: and immediately all the doors were opened, and every one's bands were loosed."
Acts 16:26

_____

_____

_____

_____

_____

_____

_____

_____

_____

_____

_____

_____

_____

_____

_____

_____

_____

_____

Writing My Way Out

CHANGE

_____

_____

_____

_____

_____

_____

_____

_____

_____

_____

_____

_____

_____

_____

_____

_____

_____

_____

_____

_____

_____

Writing My Way Out

FAITH

"And Jesus answering saith unto them, Have faith in God."
Mark 11:22

_____

_____

_____

_____

_____

_____

_____

_____

_____

_____

_____

_____

_____

_____

_____

_____

_____

_____

_____

Writing My Way Out

WORD

"For the word of the LORD is right; and all his works are done in truth."
Psalm 33:4

_____

_____

_____

_____

_____

_____

_____

_____

_____

_____

_____

_____

_____

_____

_____

_____

_____

_____

_____

Writing My Way Out

OPEN DOORS

"Ask, and it shall be given you; seek, and ye shall find;
knock, and it shall be opened unto you:"
Matthew 7:7

_____

_____

_____

_____

_____

_____

_____

_____

_____

_____

_____

_____

_____

_____

_____

_____

_____

_____

_____

_____

Writing My Way Out

CHANGE

"If a man die, shall he live again? all the days of my appointed time will I wait, till my change come."
Job 14:14

_____

_____

_____

_____

_____

_____

_____

_____

_____

_____

_____

_____

_____

_____

_____

_____

_____

_____

_____

_____

Writing My Way Out

FAITH

"Know therefore that the LORD thy God, he is God, the faithful God, which keepeth covenant and mercy with them that love him and keep his commandments to a thousand generations;"

Deuteronomy 7:9

_____

_____

_____

_____

_____

_____

_____

_____

_____

_____

_____

_____

_____

_____

_____

_____

_____

_____

Writing My Way Out

WORD

"For ever, O LORD, thy word is settled in heaven."
Psalm 119:89

_____

_____

_____

_____

_____

_____

_____

_____

_____

_____

_____

_____

_____

_____

_____

_____

_____

_____

_____

_____

_____

_____

_____

_____

Writing My Way Out

OPEN DOORS

"I am the door: by me if any man enter in, he shall be saved, and shall go in and out, and find pasture."
John 10:9

_____

_____

_____

_____

_____

_____

_____

_____

_____

_____

_____

_____

_____

_____

_____

_____

_____

_____

_____

_____

Writing My Way Out

CHANGE

"For whatever was written in former days was written for our instruction, that through endurance and through the encouragement of the Scriptures we might have hope."
Romans 15:4

_____

_____

_____

_____

_____

_____

_____

_____

_____

_____

_____

_____

_____

_____

_____

_____

_____

_____

Writing My Way Out

FAITH

"Trust in the LORD with all thine heart; and lean not unto thine own understanding."

Proverbs 3:5

_____

_____

_____

_____

_____

_____

_____

_____

_____

_____

_____

_____

_____

_____

_____

_____

_____

_____

_____

_____

_____

Writing My Way Out

WORD

*"Remember the word unto thy servant, upon which thou
hast caused me to hope."*
Psalm 119:49

_____

_____

_____

_____

_____

_____

_____

_____

_____

_____

_____

_____

_____

_____

_____

_____

_____

_____

_____

_____

_____

Writing My Way Out

OPEN DOORS

"Lift up your heads, O ye gates; and be ye lift up, ye everlasting doors; and the King of glory shall come in."
Psalm 24:7

_____

_____

_____

_____

_____

_____

_____

_____

_____

_____

_____

_____

_____

_____

_____

_____

_____

_____

_____

_____

_____

_____

Writing My Way Out

_____

_____

_____

_____

_____

_____

_____

_____

_____

_____

_____

_____

_____

_____

_____

_____

_____

_____

_____

_____

_____

_____

_____

_____

CHANGE

"Who is as the wise man? and who knoweth the interpretation of a thing? a man's wisdom maketh his face to shine, and the boldness of his face shall be changed."
Ecclesiastes 8:1

_____

_____

_____

_____

_____

_____

_____

_____

_____

_____

_____

_____

_____

_____

_____

_____

_____

_____

Writing My Way Out

FAITH

"Let us hold fast the profession of our faith without wavering; (for he is faithful that promised;)"

Hebrews 10:23

_____

_____

_____

_____

_____

_____

_____

_____

_____

_____

_____

_____

_____

_____

_____

_____

_____

_____

_____

_____

_____

Writing My Way Out

WORD

"So shall my word be that goeth forth out of my mouth: it shall not return unto me void, but it shall accomplish that which I please, and it shall prosper in the thing whereto I sent it."
Isaiah 55:11

Writing My Way Out

OPEN DOORS

"After this I looked, and, behold, a door was opened in heaven: and the first voice which I heard was as it were of a trumpet talking with me; which said, Come up hither, and I will shew thee things which must be hereafter."

Revelations 4:1

_____

_____

_____

_____

_____

_____

_____

_____

_____

_____

_____

_____

_____

_____

_____

_____

_____

_____

Writing My Way Out

CHANGE

"And now, go, write it before them on a tablet and inscribe it in a book,
that it may be for the time to come as a witness forever."
Isaiah 30:8

_____

_____

_____

_____

_____

_____

_____

_____

_____

_____

_____

_____

_____

_____

_____

_____

_____

_____

_____

Writing My Way Out

_____

_____

_____

_____

_____

_____

_____

_____

_____

_____

_____

_____

_____

_____

_____

_____

_____

_____

_____

_____

_____

_____

_____

_____

FAITH

"Cast not away therefore your confidence, which hath great recompence of reward."
Hebrews 10:35

_____

_____

_____

_____

_____

_____

_____

_____

_____

_____

_____

_____

_____

_____

_____

_____

_____

_____

_____

_____

_____

_____

Writing My Way Out

WORD

"The grass withereth, the flower fadeth: but the word of our God shall stand for ever."
Isaiah 40:8

_____

_____

_____

_____

_____

_____

_____

_____

_____

_____

_____

_____

_____

_____

_____

_____

_____

_____

_____

_____

_____

Writing My Way Out

OPEN DOORS

"But the angel of the Lord by night opened the prison doors, and brought them forth, and said, Go, stand and speak in the temple to the people all the words of this life."

Acts 5:19-20

_____

_____

_____

_____

_____

_____

_____

_____

_____

_____

_____

_____

_____

_____

_____

_____

_____

_____

_____

CHANGE

"And he changeth the times and the seasons: he removeth kings, and setteth up kings: he giveth wisdom unto the wise, and knowledge to them that know understanding:"

Daniel 2:21

_____

_____

_____

_____

_____

_____

_____

_____

_____

_____

_____

_____

_____

_____

_____

_____

_____

_____

_____

_____

Writing My Way Out

FAITH

"Yet I will rejoice in the LORD, I will joy in the God of my salvation."
Habakkuk 3:18

_____
_____
_____
_____
_____
_____
_____
_____
_____
_____
_____
_____
_____
_____
_____
_____
_____
_____
_____
_____
_____
_____
_____
_____

Writing My Way Out

_____

_____

_____

_____

_____

_____

_____

_____

_____

_____

_____

_____

_____

_____

_____

_____

_____

_____

_____

_____

_____

_____

_____

WORD

"Study to shew thyself approved unto God, a workman that needeth not to be ashamed, rightly dividing the word of truth."
2 Timothy 2:15

_____

_____

_____

_____

_____

_____

_____

_____

_____

_____

_____

_____

_____

_____

_____

_____

_____

_____

_____

_____

_____

_____

_____

Writing My Way Out

OPEN DOORS

"Stand fast therefore in the liberty wherewith Christ hath made us free, and be not entangled again with the yoke of bondage."
Galatians 5:1

_____

_____

_____

_____

_____

_____

_____

_____

_____

_____

_____

_____

_____

_____

_____

_____

_____

_____

_____

_____

_____

Writing My Way Out

CHANGE

"Out of Ephraim was there a root of them against Amalek; after thee, Benjamin, among thy people; out of Machir came down governors, and out of Zebulun they that handle the pen of the writer."

Judges 5:14

_____

_____

_____

_____

_____

_____

_____

_____

_____

_____

_____

_____

_____

_____

_____

_____

_____

_____

Writing My Way Out

FAITH

*"Now faith is the substance of things hoped for, the
evidence of things not seen."*
Hebrews 11:1

_____

_____

_____

_____

_____

_____

_____

_____

_____

_____

_____

_____

_____

_____

_____

_____

_____

_____

_____

_____

Writing My Way Out

WORD

"In God I will praise his word, in God I have put my trust; I will not fear what flesh can do unto me."

Psalm 56:4

_____

_____

_____

_____

_____

_____

_____

_____

_____

_____

_____

_____

_____

_____

_____

_____

_____

_____

_____

_____

_____

_____

_____

Writing My Way Out

OPEN DOORS

"Withal praying also for us, that God would open unto us a door of utterance, to speak the mystery of Christ, for which I am also in bonds."

Colossians 4:3

_____

_____

_____

_____

_____

_____

_____

_____

_____

_____

_____

_____

_____

_____

_____

_____

_____

_____

_____

_____

_____

Writing My Way Out

CHANGE

"But we all, with open face beholding as in a glass the glory of the Lord, are changed into the same image from glory to glory, even as by the Spirit of the Lord."
2 Corinthians 3:18

_____

_____

_____

_____

_____

_____

_____

_____

_____

_____

_____

_____

_____

_____

_____

_____

_____

_____

Writing My Way Out

FAITH

"That your faith should not stand in the wisdom of men,
but in the power of God."
1 Corinthians 2:5

Writing My Way Out

WORD

"This book of the law shall not depart out of thy mouth; but thou shalt meditate therein day and night, that thou mayest observe to do according to all that is written therein: for then thou shalt make thy way prosperous, and then thou shalt have good success."
Joshua 1:8

Writing My Way Out

OPEN DOORS

*"But the children of Israel walked upon dry land in the
midst of the sea; and the waters were a wall unto them on
their right hand, and on their left."*
Exodus 14:29

_____

_____

_____

_____

_____

_____

_____

_____

_____

_____

_____

_____

_____

_____

_____

_____

_____

_____

_____

_____

_____

_____

_____

Writing My Way Out

CHANGE

"But this shall be the covenant that I will make with the house of Israel; After those days, saith the LORD, I will put my law in their inward parts, and write it in their hearts; and will be their God, and they shall be my people."
Jeremiah 31:33

_____

_____

_____

_____

_____

_____

_____

_____

_____

_____

_____

_____

_____

_____

_____

_____

_____

_____

_____

_____

_____

_____

Writing My Way Out

FAITH

"I can do all things through Christ which strengtheneth me."
Philippians 4:13

_____

_____

_____

_____

_____

_____

_____

_____

_____

_____

_____

_____

_____

_____

_____

_____

_____

_____

_____

_____

_____

_____

_____

_____

_____

_____

_____

_____

_____

_____

_____

_____

_____

_____

_____

_____

_____

_____

_____

_____

_____

_____

_____

_____

WORD

"Is not my word like as a fire? saith the LORD; and like a hammer that breaketh the rock in pieces?"
Jeremiah 23:29

_____

_____

_____

_____

_____

_____

_____

_____

_____

_____

_____

_____

_____

_____

_____

_____

_____

_____

_____

_____

_____

Writing My Way Out

OPEN DOORS

"Behold, I stand at the door, and knock: if any man hear my voice, and open the door, I will come in to him, and will sup with him, and he with me."

Revelations 3:20

_____

_____

_____

_____

_____

_____

_____

_____

_____

_____

_____

_____

_____

_____

_____

_____

_____

_____

_____

Writing My Way Out

CHANGE

"Therefore if any man be in Christ, he is a new creature: old things are passed away; behold, all things are become new."
2 Corinthians 5:17

_____

_____

_____

_____

_____

_____

_____

_____

_____

_____

_____

_____

_____

_____

_____

_____

_____

_____

_____

_____

_____

Writing My Way Out

FAITH

"Be still, and know that I am God."
Psalm 46:10

_____

_____

_____

_____

_____

_____

_____

_____

_____

_____

_____

_____

_____

_____

_____

_____

_____

_____

_____

_____

_____

_____

Writing My Way Out

WORD

"But his delight is in the law of the LORD; and in his law doth he meditate day and night."
Psalm 1:2

_____

_____

_____

_____

_____

_____

_____

_____

_____

_____

_____

_____

_____

_____

_____

_____

_____

_____

_____

_____

_____

Writing My Way Out

OPEN DOORS

"And I will give her her vineyards from thence, and the valley of Achor for a door of hope: and she shall sing there, as in the days of her youth, and as in the day when she came up out of the land of Egypt."

Hosea 2:15

_____

_____

_____

_____

_____

_____

_____

_____

_____

_____

_____

_____

_____

_____

_____

_____

_____

_____

_____

_____

Writing My Way Out

CHANGE

"For if thou altogether holdest thy peace at this time, then shall there enlargement and deliverance arise to the Jews from another place; but thou and thy father's house shall be destroyed: and who knoweth whether thou art come to the kingdom for such a time as this?"

Esther 4:14

_____

_____

_____

_____

_____

_____

_____

_____

_____

_____

_____

_____

_____

_____

_____

_____

_____

_____

Writing My Way Out

FAITH

"For with God nothing shall be impossible."
Luke 1:37

_____

_____

_____

_____

_____

_____

_____

_____

_____

_____

_____

_____

_____

_____

_____

_____

_____

_____

_____

_____

_____

_____

Writing My Way Out

WORD

"He sent his word, and healed them, and delivered them from their destructions."
Psalm 107:20

_____

_____

_____

_____

_____

_____

_____

_____

_____

_____

_____

_____

_____

_____

_____

_____

_____

_____

_____

_____

_____

_____

_____

Writing My Way Out

_____

_____

_____

_____

_____

_____

_____

_____

_____

_____

_____

_____

_____

_____

_____

_____

_____

_____

_____

_____

_____

_____

_____

OPEN DOORS

"Though he had commanded the clouds from above, and opened the doors of heaven, And had rained down manna upon them to eat, and had given them of the corn of heaven."
Psalm 78:23-24

_____

_____

_____

_____

_____

_____

_____

_____

_____

_____

_____

_____

_____

_____

_____

_____

_____

_____

_____

_____

_____

Writing My Way Out

_____

_____

_____

_____

_____

_____

_____

_____

_____

_____

_____

_____

_____

_____

_____

_____

_____

_____

_____

_____

_____

_____

_____

_____

_____

_____

CHANGE

*"Every good gift and every perfect gift is from above,
and cometh down from the Father of lights, with whom
is no variableness, neither shadow of turning."*

James 1:17

_____

_____

_____

_____

_____

_____

_____

_____

_____

_____

_____

_____

_____

_____

_____

_____

_____

_____

_____

_____

_____

Writing My Way Out

FAITH

"Fear thou not; for I am with thee: be not dismayed;
for I am thy God."
Isaiah 41:10

_____

_____

_____

_____

_____

_____

_____

_____

_____

_____

_____

_____

_____

_____

_____

_____

_____

_____

_____

_____

_____

_____

Writing My Way Out

WORD

"Jesus answered and said unto him, If a man love me, he will keep my words: and my Father will love him, and we will come unto him, and make our abode with him."

John 14:23

_____

_____

_____

_____

_____

_____

_____

_____

_____

_____

_____

_____

_____

_____

_____

_____

_____

_____

_____

_____

Writing My Way Out

OPEN DOORS

"Then the same day at evening, being the first day of the week, when the doors were shut where the disciples were assembled for fear of the Jews, came Jesus and stood in the midst, and saith unto them, Peace be unto you."
John 20:19

_____

_____

_____

_____

_____

_____

_____

_____

_____

_____

_____

_____

_____

_____

_____

_____

_____

_____

_____

_____

Writing My Way Out

CHANGE

"My heart is inditing a good matter: I speak of the things which I have made touching the king: my tongue is the pen of a ready writer."
Psalm 45:1

_____

_____

_____

_____

_____

_____

_____

_____

_____

_____

_____

_____

_____

_____

_____

_____

_____

_____

_____

_____

Writing My Way Out

_____

_____

_____

_____

_____

_____

_____

_____

_____

_____

_____

_____

_____

_____

_____

_____

_____

_____

_____

_____

_____

_____

_____

_____

FAITH

"But without faith it is impossible to please him: for he that cometh to God must believe that he is, and that he is a rewarder of them that diligently seek him."

Hebrews 11:6

Writing My Way Out

WORD

"Thou shalt also decree a thing, and it shall be established unto thee: and the light shall shine upon thy ways."

Job 22:28

Writing My Way Out

OPEN DOORS

"And he saith unto him, Verily, verily, I say unto you, Hereafter ye shall see heaven open, and the angels of God ascending and descending upon the Son of man."

John 1:51

_____

_____

_____

_____

_____

_____

_____

_____

_____

_____

_____

_____

_____

_____

_____

_____

_____

_____

_____

_____

_____

Writing My Way Out

_____

_____

_____

_____

_____

_____

_____

_____

_____

_____

_____

_____

_____

_____

_____

_____

_____

_____

_____

_____

_____

_____

_____

_____

_____

CHANGE

"For our light affliction, which is but for a moment, worketh for us a far more exceeding and eternal weight of glory;"
2 Corinthians 4:17

_____

_____

_____

_____

_____

_____

_____

_____

_____

_____

_____

_____

_____

_____

_____

_____

_____

_____

_____

_____

FAITH

"By faith the walls of Jericho fell down, after they were
compassed about seven days."
Hebrews 11:30

_____

_____

_____

_____

_____

_____

_____

_____

_____

_____

_____

_____

_____

_____

_____

_____

_____

_____

_____

_____

Writing My Way Out

WORD

"How forcible are right words! but what doth your arguing reprove?"
Job 6:25

Writing My Way Out

OPEN DOORS

"Thus saith the LORD to his anointed, to Cyrus, whose right hand I have holden, to subdue nations before him; and I will loose the loins of kings, to open before him the two leaved gates; and the gates shall not be shut;"
Isaiah 45:1

_____

_____

_____

_____

_____

_____

_____

_____

_____

_____

_____

_____

_____

_____

_____

_____

_____

_____

_____

_____

Writing My Way Out

CHANGE

"Let not mercy and truth forsake thee: bind them about thy neck; write them upon the table of thine heart:"
Proverbs 3:3

_____

_____

_____

_____

_____

_____

_____

_____

_____

_____

_____

_____

_____

_____

_____

_____

_____

_____

_____

_____

_____

Writing My Way Out

FAITH

"For in it the righteousness of God is revealed from faith for faith, as it is written, "The righteous shall live by faith.""
Romans 1:17

Writing My Way Out

WORD

"Being confident of this very thing, that he which hath begun a good work in you will perform it until the day of Jesus Christ:"
Philippians 1:6

_____

_____

_____

_____

_____

_____

_____

_____

_____

_____

_____

_____

_____

_____

_____

_____

_____

_____

_____

_____

_____

_____

_____

Writing My Way Out

OPEN DOORS

"And I will give unto thee the keys of the kingdom of heaven: and whatsoever thou shalt bind on earth shall be bound in heaven: and whatsoever thou shalt loose on earth shall be loosed in heaven."
Matthew 16:19

Writing My Way Out

CHANGE

"Beloved, now are we the sons of God, and it doth not yet appear what we shall be: but we know that, when he shall appear, we shall be like him; for we shall see him as he is."

1 John 3:2

_____

_____

_____

_____

_____

_____

_____

_____

_____

_____

_____

_____

_____

_____

_____

_____

_____

_____

_____

_____

_____

Writing My Way Out

_____

_____

_____

_____

_____

_____

_____

_____

_____

_____

_____

_____

_____

_____

_____

_____

_____

_____

_____

_____

_____

_____

_____

_____

_____

_____

FAITH

"Fight the good fight of faith."
1Timothy 6:12

WORD

"Then the LORD put forth his hand, and touched my mouth. And the LORD said unto me, Behold, I have put my words in thy mouth."
Jeremiah 1:9

Writing My Way Out

_____

_____

_____

_____

_____

_____

_____

_____

_____

_____

_____

_____

_____

_____

_____

_____

_____

_____

_____

_____

_____

_____

_____

_____

OPEN DOORS

"Jesus saith unto him, I am the way, the truth, and the life: no man cometh unto the Father, but by me."
John 14:6

_____

_____

_____

_____

_____

_____

_____

_____

_____

_____

_____

_____

_____

_____

_____

_____

_____

_____

_____

Writing My Way Out

CHANGE

"Behold, I will do a new thing; now it shall spring forth;
shall ye not know it? I will even make a way in the
wilderness, and rivers in the desert."
Isaiah 43:19

_____

_____

_____

_____

_____

_____

_____

_____

_____

_____

_____

_____

_____

_____

_____

_____

_____

_____

_____

Writing My Way Out

_____

_____

_____

_____

_____

_____

_____

_____

_____

_____

_____

_____

_____

_____

_____

_____

_____

_____

_____

_____

_____

_____

_____

Made in the USA
Columbia, SC
21 March 2024

33113202R00095